Horoscope 2024

Astrological Guide for Prosperity and a Successful Year.

Insights and Keys to Health, Love, and Destiny.

Susan Nicholas

© **Copyright 2023 all rights reserved**.

This document is geared towards providing exact and reliable information with regard to the topic and issue covered. The publication is sold with the idea that the publisher is not required to render accounting, officially permitted, or otherwise qualified services. If advice is necessary, legal or professional, a practiced individual in the profession should be ordered.

From a Declaration of Principles which was accepted and approved equally by a Committee of the American Bar Association and a Committee of Publishers and Associations.

In no way is it legal to reproduce, duplicate, or transmit any part of this document in either electronic means or in printed format. Recording of this publication is strictly prohibited, and any storage of this document is not allowed unless with written permission from the publisher. All rights reserved.

The information provided herein is stated to be truthful and consistent, in that any liability, in terms of inattention or otherwise, by any usage or abuse of any policies, processes, or directions contained within is the solitary and utter responsibility of the recipient reader. Under no circumstances will any legal responsibility or blame be held against the publisher for any reparation, damages, or monetary loss due to the information herein, either directly or indirectly.

Table of Contents:

Chapter 1: Introduction 1
    Overview of Astrology for the Year 2024 1
    Planetary Movements and Their Impact on Predictions 3
    Zodiac Sign Overviews – Key Traits and Characteristics 6

Chapter 2: Monthly Forecasts for Each Zodiac Sign 9
    Navigating the Year Ahead: Month-by-Month Insights 9
    Focus on love, career, health, and personal well-being 32
    Custom advice for facing challenges and seizing opportunities 38

Chapter 3: Love and Relationships 42
    Analyzing Sign Compatibilities for 2024 42
    Nurturing Healthy and Fulfilling Relationships 45
    Favorable Periods for New Encounters and Significant Decisions ... 48

Chapter 4: Career and Finance 53
    Forecasts for Career and Financial Advancement 53
    Auspicious Times to Launch Projects or Make Investments 57
    Money Management Tips for 2024 Based on Your Zodiac Sign 61

Chapter 5: Health and Wellness 64
    Lifestyle and Wellness Tips for 2024 Tailored to Each Zodiac Sign ... 64
    Critical Periods for Health and Prevention Strategies in 2024 68
    The Importance of Mental and Physical Balance in 2024 71

Chapter 6: Personal Transformation and Spiritual Growth 75
    Overcoming Personal Obstacles and Embracing Inner Growth 75
    Significant Astrological Moments for Personal Transformation 79
    Recommended Meditations and Spiritual Practices for 2024 83

Chapter 7: Retrograde Planets and Their Impact on 2024 87
    Explanation of Retrograde Periods of Planets 87

Retrograde Planets and Their Impact on 2024 90

Chapter 8: Key Astral Events of 2024 93

Eclipses, Conjunctions, and Significant Astral Events 93

Key Astral Events of 2024 for Zodiac Signs 97

Chapter 9: Overcoming Misfortune in 2024 101

Lucky Numbers, Days, and More for Each Zodiac Sign 101

Chapter 10: Conclusion 105

Embracing 2024 with a Proactive Approach 105

Awareness and Personal Growth through Astrology in 2024 107

How to Use the Horoscope for Personal Planning in 2024 110

Chapter 1: Introduction
Overview of Astrology for the Year 2024

Welcome to "Horoscope 2024: Astrological Guide for a Successful Year." In this book, we embark on a celestial journey through the year 2024, exploring the profound impact of astrology on our daily lives. As we turn each page, we delve into the intricate tapestry of cosmic influences that shape our experiences, decisions, and personal growth.

The year 2024 marks a significant period in the astrological calendar, characterized by dynamic planetary alignments and movements. These celestial phenomena offer a unique lens through which we can view and navigate the complexities of our lives. In this guide, we will explore the roles and influences of various celestial bodies, from the assertive energy of Mars to the transformative orbit of Pluto.

Astrology, an ancient practice rich in symbolism and meaning, extends far beyond simple horoscopes. It is a nuanced language of the stars, offering insights into the interconnectedness of the universe and our place within it. As we journey through 2024, this book will serve as your companion, illuminating the paths the stars have charted for us.

Each zodiac sign will be explored in depth, providing a thorough understanding of the unique characteristics and tendencies that define them. Whether you are a passionate Leo, a thoughtful Gemini, or a resilient Capricorn, this book aims to shed light on the personal journey that awaits you in 2024.

We will meticulously dissect key astrological events of the year, including planetary transits, retrogrades, and significant eclipses. These cosmic occurrences are not merely astronomical phenomena; they hold the keys to understanding our inner transformations, relationships, career paths, and overall wellbeing.

This book is not a tool for predicting the future; rather, it offers a framework for understanding the potential and possibilities that lie ahead. By aligning ourselves with the cosmic rhythms, we gain the clarity and wisdom to make choices that resonate with our deepest truths and aspirations.

As you immerse yourself in the pages of this guide, approach it with curiosity and an open spirit. The insights contained within are meant to inspire reflection, self-awareness, and a deeper connection with the cosmos. Let this knowledge be your guide as you navigate the year 2024, a year brimming with opportunities for personal discovery, growth, and transformation.

Together, let's explore the rich and enigmatic world of astrology as it unfolds in the year 2024.

Planetary Movements and Their Impact on Predictions

The Dance of the Planets: Understanding their Significance in Astrology

In the intricate world of astrology, the movements of the planets are like the rhythm of a cosmic dance, each step and turn resonating through our lives. This chapter delves into the significance of these celestial movements and how they shape the predictions and insights we glean from astrology.

The Role of Each Planet

Each planet in our solar system plays a unique role in astrology, representing different aspects of our lives and personalities. For instance, Mercury governs communication and intellect, Venus oversees love and beauty, while Mars symbolizes action and energy. Understanding the nature and domain of each planet helps us comprehend how their movements can impact us on a personal level.

Planetary Transits and Their Effects

A transit occurs when a planet moves into a new position in the sky, forming an angle with the position of a planet in our natal chart. These transits are the key drivers of change and growth in our lives. For example, when Jupiter transits, it brings expansion and growth in the area it touches, while Saturn's transit often signals a time of challenge and discipline.

Retrogrades: Times of Reflection

Retrograde periods, when planets appear to move backward in the sky, are significant in astrology. These times are often associated with introspection and revisiting past themes. Mercury retrograde is famous for communication breakdowns and travel mishaps, encouraging us to slow down and rethink our plans and ideas.

The Impact of Major Alignments

Conjunctions, oppositions, and squares between planets create powerful energies that can significantly influence our lives. These alignments can herald times of tension, harmony, or transformation, depending on the planets involved and their aspects. For example, a conjunction between Venus and Mars might ignite passionate love affairs, while a square between the Moon and Neptune could lead to emotional confusion.

Eclipses: Moments of Destiny

Eclipses, both solar and lunar, are pivotal moments in astrology. They often mark significant beginnings and endings, times when the universe seems to realign our paths. Eclipses can bring unexpected events, revealing hidden truths and redirecting our journey in profound ways.

The Big Picture: Outer Planets and Generational Influence

The slower-moving outer planets – Jupiter, Saturn, Uranus, Neptune, and Pluto – have a generational impact, shaping broader social trends and collective experiences. Their transits mark significant epochs in human history and evolution, influencing the collective mindset and major world events.

Personalizing the Planetary Movements

While understanding the general influence of planetary movements is fascinating, the true power of astrology lies in personalization. By examining these movements in relation to your natal chart, you can gain specific insights into how these cosmic shifts will affect you personally, guiding you toward greater self-awareness and alignment with your life's purpose.

In conclusion, the dance of the planets is a complex and beautiful symphony that influences our lives in myriad ways. By understanding and respecting these celestial movements, we can harness their energies to guide us in our journey through life.

Zodiac Sign Overviews – Key Traits and Characteristics

Embarking on a Zodiac Journey: Understanding the Twelve Signs

In this chapter, we explore the fundamental essence of each of the twelve zodiac signs. Astrology offers a rich tapestry of characteristics, tendencies, and potentialities that are believed to be influenced by the position of the sun at the time of birth. These signs provide a framework for understanding our personalities, behaviors, and life paths.

1. Aries (March 21 - April 19)

- Element: Fire
- Traits: Energetic, courageous, and independent. Aries are known for their leadership qualities and a zest for life. They are often driven and competitive, with a strong desire to be first.

2. Taurus (April 20 - May 20)

- Element: Earth
- Traits: Reliable, patient, and practical. Taureans appreciate the finer things in life and are known for their sensuality. They value stability and are often very determined.

3. Gemini (May 21 - June 20)

- Element: Air
- Traits: Curious, adaptable, and communicative. Geminis are quick-witted and sociable, often with a love for variety and intellectual stimulation.

4. Cancer (June 21 - July 22)

- Element: Water
- Traits: Intuitive, emotional, and nurturing. Cancers are deeply sensitive and caring, with a strong connection to home and family.

5. Leo (July 23 - August 22)

- Element: Fire
- Traits: Confident, generous, and charismatic. Leos love to be in the spotlight and are known for their creativity and leadership.

6. Virgo (August 23 - September 22)

- Element: Earth
- Traits: Analytical, meticulous, and practical. Virgos are often perfectionists, with a keen eye for detail and a strong sense of duty.

7. Libra (September 23 - October 22)

- Element: Air

- Traits: Diplomatic, fair-minded, and sociable. Libras seek harmony and balance, often excelling in relationships and artistic pursuits.

8. Scorpio (October 23 - November 21)

- Element: Water
- Traits: Passionate, resourceful, and intense. Scorpios are known for their emotional depth and powerful presence.

9. Sagittarius (November 22 - December 21)

- Element: Fire
- Traits: Adventurous, optimistic, and freedom-loving. Sagittarians are known for their love of travel and quest for knowledge.

10. Capricorn (December 22 - January 19) - Element: Earth - Traits: Ambitious, disciplined, and practical. Capricorns are determined and often excel in their professional lives.

11. Aquarius (January 20 - February 18) - Element: Air - Traits: Innovative, independent, and humanitarian. Aquarians are forward-thinking and often concerned with larger societal issues.

12. Pisces (February 19 - March 20) - Element: Water - Traits: Compassionate, artistic, and intuitive. Pisces are known for their empathy and often have a strong connection to the arts and spirituality.

As we journey through each sign, it's important to remember that astrology is a complex and nuanced field. Each individual is unique, and their astrological profile is influenced by a multitude of factors beyond their sun sign. However, these general characteristics offer a starting point for understanding the basic qualities associated with each sign.

Chapter 2: Monthly Forecasts for Each Zodiac Sign

Navigating the Year Ahead: Month-by-Month Insights

In this chapter, we present a comprehensive guide to the astrological influences that each zodiac sign can expect to encounter throughout 2024. These detailed month-by-month forecasts offer insights into the opportunities and challenges that may arise, helping you navigate the year with greater understanding and foresight.

Aries (March 21 - April 19)

- **January**: A time for new beginnings. Your energy is high, making it an ideal time to start new projects. Set

your goals high and initiate plans that you've been pondering.
- **February**: Focus on relationships. Valentine's Day may bring a significant development in your love life. This is a great time for deepening existing relationships or starting a new one.
- **March**: Your career comes into focus. Opportunities for advancement and new projects may present themselves. Be ready to take the lead and show your capabilities.
- **April**: Financial matters require attention. Look into budgeting and saving plans. This could be a good time to make a significant investment or financial decision.
- **May**: A shift towards personal growth and self-improvement. Consider picking up a new hobby or starting a fitness regimen. Mental and physical health are in the spotlight.
- **June**: Social activities and networking are favored. Attend events and connect with new groups. These interactions could lead to important future collaborations.
- **July**: Family matters may require more attention. There could be a family gathering or a need to address home-related issues. Focus on balancing work and home life.
- **August**: Creative energies are high. This is a good month for artistic pursuits or any creative projects. Your innovative ideas will be well-received.
- **September**: Travel opportunities may arise. Whether it's for work or pleasure, these trips could offer valuable life experiences and a chance for personal reflection.

- **October**: A period of introspection and self-discovery. Take time to reflect on your personal journey and inner growth. Spiritual or meditative practices could be beneficial.
- **November**: Career achievements could peak this month. Your hard work is likely to be recognized, potentially leading to a promotion or new job opportunities.
- **December**: The focus returns to relationships. The holiday season is a time for connection and warmth. Strengthen your bonds with loved ones and enjoy festive celebrations.

This forecast for Aries in 2024 suggests a year filled with growth, opportunities, and the chance to strengthen relationships. As always, these astrological insights are guides and not absolutes, offering pathways to navigate the year's challenges and opportunities.

Taurus (April 20 - May 20)

- **January**: Financial planning is key. Look for opportunities to increase your income, possibly through investments or a new business venture. It's a good time to review and adjust your budget.
- **February**: Your social life picks up. Enjoy the company of friends and family. This is a great month for networking and strengthening your connections.

- **March**: Focus on personal development. You might find yourself interested in learning a new skill or pursuing a new hobby. Education and self-improvement are highlighted.
- **April**: Health and wellness come into focus. Consider starting a new exercise routine or revamping your diet. It's a time to prioritize your physical and mental well-being.
- **May**: Your birthday month brings a surge of energy and confidence. It's a time for celebration and personal reflection. Set intentions for the coming year.
- **June**: Career opportunities may arise. Be ready to take on new responsibilities or consider a career change. Your hard work is likely to be recognized.
- **July**: Travel could be on the horizon. Whether it's a vacation or a work-related trip, embrace the opportunity to explore new places and cultures.
- **August**: Relationships, both romantic and platonic, come into the spotlight. This is a time for deepening connections and possibly meeting someone special if you're single.
- **September**: Financial matters need attention again. You may see the results of your earlier financial planning. Keep an eye on investments and savings.
- **October**: Home and family matters may require your focus. Consider home improvements or spending quality time with family. Balance is key.

- **November**: Creativity is heightened. Engage in artistic activities or creative projects. It's also a good time for social events and entertainment.
- **December**: The year ends with a focus on introspection and planning for the future. Reflect on the past year and set goals for the next. It's a time for closure and new beginnings.

This forecast for Taurus in 2024 suggests a year of personal growth, financial opportunities, and strengthening relationships. Remember, these astrological insights are meant to provide guidance and perspective, and the path you choose is ultimately yours to create.

Gemini (May 21 - June 20)

- **January**: Creative pursuits are favored. This is an excellent time to express yourself artistically. Whether it's writing, painting, or any other form of art, your creative juices are flowing.
- **February**: Communication is crucial. Focus on clear and effective communication, especially in your personal and professional relationships. Clear up any misunderstandings and engage in honest conversations.
- **March**: A focus on home and family. You might find yourself spending more time at home or with family

members. It's a great period for home improvement projects or family gatherings.
- **April**: Your social circle expands. New friendships and networking opportunities arise. Engage in social events and community activities to meet like-minded individuals.
- **May**: Personal growth is highlighted. You may feel motivated to embark on a journey of self-discovery or personal development. Consider taking up courses or reading to expand your knowledge.
- **June**: Career and professional life come into focus. This could be a pivotal time for career advancement or starting a new business venture. Be ready to seize opportunities.
- **July**: Financial management is key. Pay attention to your finances, budgeting, and investments. It's a good time to plan for future financial security.
- **August**: Love and relationships take the spotlight. If you are single, you might meet someone special. For those in a relationship, this is a time to rekindle romance.
- **September**: Health and wellness are important. Focus on maintaining a healthy lifestyle. Incorporate regular exercise and balanced nutrition into your daily routine.
- **October**: Travel is on the cards. Plan a trip or a vacation. It could be an excellent opportunity for relaxation and gaining new perspectives.
- **November**: Reflection and introspection. Spend time contemplating your life's direction and goals. Journaling or meditative practices could be beneficial.

- **December**: The year ends with a focus on celebration and joy. It's a time to enjoy the festive season with friends and family, reflecting on the year's achievements and looking forward to the future.

The forecast for Gemini in 2024 suggests a year filled with opportunities for creative expression, personal growth, and strengthening relationships. As with any astrological prediction, these insights are meant to guide and inspire rather than dictate your path. Use them to navigate the year with optimism and a sense of exploration.

Cancer (June 21 - July 22)

- **January**: Focus on self-care. This month is about rejuvenating your mind and body. Prioritize activities that bring relaxation and wellness, such as yoga or meditation.
- **February**: Home and family take center stage. Organize a family gathering or invest time in home improvement projects. It's a period for strengthening family bonds.
- **March**: Creativity and hobbies are highlighted. Engage in activities that fuel your artistic talents or start a new creative project. It's a time to let your imagination run wild.
- **April**: Professional life demands attention. Opportunities for career advancement may arise. Stay open to new challenges and be prepared to take on leadership roles.

- **May**: Social life becomes active. Attend events, reconnect with old friends, and make new acquaintances. Networking can lead to exciting opportunities.
- **June**: Focus on financial planning. Review your budget, consider investments, and plan for future financial security. It's a good time to seek financial advice if needed.
- **July**: Travel and adventure call. Plan a vacation or a short trip to recharge. Exploring new places can bring new perspectives and inspiration.
- **August**: Relationships, both romantic and platonic, are in focus. If single, you might meet someone special. For those in relationships, deepen your connection with your partner.
- **September**: Health and wellness are important. Pay attention to your physical and mental well-being. Implementing a new fitness routine or diet plan could be beneficial.
- **October**: Career opportunities may present themselves again. Be ready to showcase your skills and talents. A promotion or a new job offer could be on the horizon.
- **November**: Personal growth and self-reflection are key. Take time to assess your life's path and goals. Consider engaging in spiritual or self-improvement activities.
- **December**: The year ends with a focus on introspection and family. Enjoy the holiday season with your loved ones and reflect on the year's achievements and future aspirations.

The forecast for Cancer in 2024 suggests a year filled with opportunities for personal and professional growth, deepening relationships, and focusing on self-care. These astrological insights are intended to guide and assist in navigating the year's challenges and opportunities. Remember, the choices and paths you take are ultimately yours.

Leo (July 23 - August 22)

- **January**: Leadership opportunities emerge. This is a time to step into roles that allow you to shine and demonstrate your capabilities. Your natural charisma and confidence attract positive attention.
- **February**: Romance is in the air. Plan a special date or outing, especially around Valentine's Day. If you're single, you might meet someone who captures your heart. For those in relationships, rekindle the passion.
- **March**: Creative projects flourish. Your creative energy is high, making it an ideal time to start or complete artistic endeavors. This is also a good period for hobbies and leisure activities.
- **April**: Focus on home and family. There may be events or situations that require your attention at home. It's a great time to connect with family members and create lasting memories.
- **May**: Career takes center stage. You may be presented with new job opportunities or projects that challenge and excite you. Your leadership skills are in demand.

- **June**: Time for self-reflection and personal growth. Consider your long-term goals and aspirations. It's a good month for planning and strategizing your future.
- **July**: Birthday month brings renewal and celebration. Reflect on the past year and set intentions for the new one. It's a time of personal significance and joyous gatherings.
- **August**: Financial focus. Review your finances, consider investments, and look for ways to improve your financial stability. It might be a good time to seek advice from financial experts.
- **September**: Social activities are highlighted. Attend events, parties, and gatherings. This is a perfect time to expand your social circle and make new connections.
- **October**: Travel may be on the horizon. Whether it's for work or leisure, traveling this month can provide a refreshing change of pace and new experiences.
- **November**: Health and wellness come into focus. Pay attention to your physical fitness and mental well-being. Implementing a new health regimen could be beneficial.
- **December**: The year ends with introspection and planning. Reflect on your achievements and set goals for the coming year. It's also a time to relax and enjoy the holiday season with loved ones.

This forecast for Leo in 2024 suggests a year filled with opportunities for leadership, creativity, and personal growth. Remember, these astrological insights are intended to provide guidance and help you make the most of the year's potential. Your individual choices and actions will shape your journey.

Virgo (August 23 - September 22)

- **January**: Health and fitness are highlighted. This is a perfect time to start a new wellness routine or revamp your diet. Focus on activities that improve both your physical and mental well-being.
- **February**: Career advancements are possible. Stay focused on your professional goals. Hard work and dedication might lead to significant achievements or recognition at your workplace.
- **March**: Financial planning requires attention. Look at your budget and savings, and consider making smart investments for long-term benefits. It's a good period for financial strategizing.
- **April**: Social life becomes vibrant. Engage more with friends and expand your social network. It's also a favorable time for collaborative projects and team efforts.
- **May**: Personal relationships come into focus. Whether it's strengthening existing relationships or forging new ones, this month is about connecting with others on a deeper level.

- **June**: Travel opportunities may arise. Whether for leisure or work, travel can bring new experiences and broaden your horizons. Embrace the chance to explore.
- **July**: Creativity and hobbies are encouraged. Indulge in activities that fuel your creative side. Whether it's arts, crafts, or a new hobby, let your imagination run free.
- **August**: Your birthday month brings introspection and self-reflection. Consider your achievements and set goals for the new year. It's a time for personal growth and setting new intentions.
- **September**: Education and learning are in the spotlight. Consider taking up a course or workshop to enhance your skills. It's an excellent time for intellectual pursuits and expanding your knowledge.
- **October**: Home and family matters may require your attention. This could involve home improvement projects or family events. Strive for balance between your personal and professional life.
- **November**: Spiritual and emotional well-being come into focus. Engage in activities that nurture your soul, like meditation, yoga, or spending time in nature.
- **December**: The year ends with a focus on celebration and reflection. Enjoy the festive season, and take time to appreciate the year's journey. It's also a great period to plan for the upcoming year.

This forecast for Virgo in 2024 suggests a year filled with opportunities for personal and professional growth, health improvement, and deepening relationships. These astrological insights are intended to guide you in making the most of the year's potential, shaping your journey according to your personal goals and aspirations.

Libra (September 23 - October 22)

- **January**: Balance is your mantra. This month, strive for equilibrium in all areas of your life. Focus on maintaining a healthy work-life balance and nurturing your relationships.
- **February**: Legal matters may come to the forefront. Address them with clarity and precision. It's also a good time to resolve any pending disputes or negotiations.
- **March**: Your social circle expands. Engage in new activities and meet new people. Networking can lead to exciting opportunities both personally and professionally.
- **April**: Focus on personal development. This is a great time for self-improvement, whether it's learning a new skill or enhancing your knowledge.
- **May**: Career opportunities emerge. Be ready to take on new challenges at work. Your diplomatic skills and fair approach make you a valuable team player.
- **June**: Financial planning is highlighted. Review your investments and budget. Consider seeking advice from a financial expert to optimize your finances.

- **July**: Travel opportunities arise. Whether it's for leisure or work, travel can bring new insights and broaden your horizons. Embrace new experiences.
- **August**: Relationships are in focus. This is a good time to work on your existing relationships and, if single, to be open to new romantic possibilities.
- **September**: Health and wellness should be a priority. Pay attention to your physical and mental well-being. Start a new health regimen or refine your current one.
- **October**: Your birthday month brings introspection and goal-setting. Reflect on the past year and plan for the future. Celebrate your achievements with loved ones.
- **November**: Creativity and hobbies take center stage. Indulge in artistic pursuits or start a new creative project. This can be a source of joy and relaxation.
- **December**: The year ends with a focus on family and home. Enjoy the holiday season and cherish the time spent with family and friends. It's also a good period for home improvement projects.

This forecast for Libra in 2024 suggests a year filled with opportunities for growth, balancing personal and professional life, and strengthening relationships. Use these astrological insights as a guide to navigate the year, making choices that align with your values and aspirations.

Scorpio (October 23 - November 21)

- **January**: Introspection and personal growth are themes. It's a time to explore your inner world and possibly confront some deep-seated issues. Meditative practices and journaling can be beneficial.
- **February**: Financial gains are possible. Look for investment opportunities and ways to enhance your financial stability. It's also a good time to review your financial plans and make necessary adjustments.
- **March**: Social life becomes vibrant. Reconnect with old friends and be open to making new connections. Your social network could bring valuable opportunities.
- **April**: Focus on career and professional development. You might be recognized for your hard work or be presented with new job opportunities. Be prepared to take on new challenges.
- **May**: Romance and relationships come into focus. If single, you might find a meaningful connection. For those in relationships, it's a time to deepen your bond.
- **June**: Health and wellness are highlighted. Prioritize your physical and mental well-being. This might involve starting a new fitness routine or diet.
- **July**: Travel opportunities arise. Whether it's for leisure or work, embrace the chance to explore new places and cultures. Travel could bring valuable life lessons and insights.

- **August**: Creative projects and hobbies are encouraged. Express yourself through art, writing, or other creative outlets. This is a time to let your creativity shine.
- **September**: Education and learning are in the spotlight. Consider enrolling in a course or attending workshops to enhance your skills or knowledge.
- **October**: Your birthday month brings reflection and self-evaluation. Consider the progress you've made and set goals for the coming year. It's a period for both celebration and planning.
- **November**: Family and home life take center stage. Spend quality time with family members and focus on improving your living space. It's a time for nurturing your personal life.
- **December**: The year ends with a focus on relaxation and rejuvenation. Take time to unwind and enjoy the holiday season. Reflect on the year's experiences and prepare for the new year ahead.

This forecast for Scorpio in 2024 suggests a year filled with opportunities for introspection, financial growth, and deepening personal connections. Remember, these astrological insights are intended to guide you through the year, helping you make the most of its potential. Your personal choices will ultimately shape your experiences.

Sagittarius (November 22 - December 21)

- **January**: Travel opportunities may arise. It's a perfect time to expand your horizons, whether through physical journeys or exploring new ideas and cultures. Embrace adventure and new experiences.
- **February**: Education and learning are favored. Consider enrolling in a course, workshop, or perhaps a seminar that piques your interest. It's an excellent period for intellectual growth.
- **March**: Networking and social interactions are highlighted. Attend social events, engage in community activities, and expand your social circle. These connections can open doors to new opportunities.
- **April**: Focus on career development. You may encounter opportunities for advancement or discover a new path that aligns more closely with your passions.
- **May**: Financial planning is key. Review and adjust your financial strategies, look for investment opportunities, and manage your resources wisely.
- **June**: Romance and personal relationships come into focus. If you're single, you might meet someone special. If you're in a relationship, deepen your connection with your partner.
- **July**: Health and wellness are important. Implement a new fitness regimen or focus on healthier lifestyle choices. Pay attention to both your physical and mental health.

- **August**: Creative projects and self-expression are encouraged. This is a great time to engage in artistic activities or to start a project you've been contemplating.
- **September**: Family and home life gain importance. Spend quality time with family members, or you might consider making some changes or improvements in your home environment.
- **October**: Travel may once again be in the cards. Plan a trip or a vacation, especially one that involves exploring places off the beaten path.
- **November**: Reflect on your personal growth and achievements. As your birthday approaches, review the past year and set intentions for the coming one.
- **December**: The year ends with a focus on relaxation and enjoying the holiday season. Spend time with friends and family, and celebrate your accomplishments.

This forecast for Sagittarius in 2024 suggests a year filled with opportunities for adventure, personal growth, and expanding your horizons. These astrological insights are meant to guide and inspire you throughout the year, helping you to make the most of the opportunities that come your way.

Capricorn (December 22 - January 19)

- **January**: Professional achievements are in focus. Aim high in your career aspirations. It's a great time to set

ambitious goals and work towards them with determination.
- **February**: Networking is key. Connect with influential individuals and explore new opportunities for collaboration. Attend professional events and engage in meaningful conversations.
- **March**: Financial planning and management take priority. Review your investments and consider long-term financial strategies. It's also a good time to seek advice from financial experts.
- **April**: Personal development and self-improvement are highlighted. Consider enrolling in a course or seeking new learning experiences that can enhance your skills.
- **May**: Balance between work and personal life is crucial. Make time for relaxation and activities that rejuvenate you. Pay attention to your well-being.
- **June**: Creative projects and hobbies may pique your interest. Pursue activities that allow you to express your creativity and provide a break from your routine.
- **July**: Travel opportunities may arise. Whether it's for business or pleasure, traveling can offer new perspectives and a chance to recharge.
- **August**: Relationships, both personal and professional, come into focus. Strengthen your connections and communicate effectively to build trust and understanding.
- **September**: Health and fitness should be a priority. Implement a new health regimen or refine your current one. Focus on maintaining a healthy lifestyle.

- **October**: Career development and growth continue to be significant. Take on new challenges at work and demonstrate your leadership and problem-solving skills.
- **November**: Reflect on your personal and professional growth. As your birthday approaches, assess the progress made and set goals for the coming year.
- **December**: The year ends with a focus on family and celebrations. Enjoy the holiday season, spend time with loved ones, and cherish these moments.

This forecast for Capricorn in 2024 suggests a year filled with opportunities for professional growth, financial management, and personal development. Use these astrological insights to guide your decisions and actions throughout the year, aligning them with your long-term goals and aspirations.

Aquarius (January 20 - February 18)

- **January**: Embrace innovation and change. This is an excellent time to think outside the box and explore new ideas. Be open to adopting new technologies or methods in both your personal and professional life.
- **February**: Community involvement brings joy. Participate in local events or volunteer activities. Your contributions can make a significant impact and bring a sense of fulfillment.

- **March**: Focus on personal relationships. This is a time to strengthen your connections with friends and family. Communication and understanding are key.
- **April**: Career and professional development are in the spotlight. You might encounter opportunities for advancement or new projects that challenge and inspire you.
- **May**: Financial planning is essential. Review your investments and savings strategies. Consider consulting with a financial advisor to make the most of your resources.
- **June**: Travel opportunities may arise. This is a great time for both leisure and exploration. Travel can provide new perspectives and inspiration.
- **July**: Creativity and self-expression are encouraged. Engage in artistic activities or hobbies that allow you to express your unique ideas and personality.
- **August**: Health and wellness should be a priority. Implement new health routines, focus on nutrition, and make time for physical activity.
- **September**: Education and learning are highlighted. Consider enrolling in a course or attending a seminar that aligns with your interests or career goals.
- **October**: Focus on home and family. This might involve home improvements or spending quality time with family members. It's a time for nurturing your personal life.
- **November**: Social activities and networking are important. Attend social events, meet new people, and

expand your social circle. These connections can lead to exciting opportunities.
- **December**: The year ends with introspection and planning for the future. Reflect on the past year's achievements and set goals for the upcoming year. It's a time for renewal and setting new intentions.

This forecast for Aquarius in 2024 suggests a year filled with opportunities for growth, innovation, and strengthening community and personal connections. Use these astrological insights to guide your decisions and actions throughout the year, aligning them with your vision for the future.

Pisces (February 19 - March 20)

- **January**: Creative inspiration flows. This is an excellent time to engage in artistic activities. Whether it's painting, writing, music, or any other form of art, your creativity is at a peak.
- **February**: Emotional connections deepen. Spend quality time with loved ones. It's a period for strengthening your relationships and forming deeper bonds.
- **March**: Focus on personal growth and self-improvement. Consider taking up new hobbies or learning new skills that contribute to your personal development.

- **April**: Career and professional life may bring new opportunities. Be open to new challenges and projects that can advance your career aspirations.
- **May**: Financial planning and management are important. Review your budget, savings, and investment plans. It's a good time to make informed financial decisions.
- **June**: Travel opportunities may present themselves. Whether for leisure or exploration, traveling can offer new experiences and broaden your perspectives.
- **July**: Health and wellness come into focus. Prioritize your physical and mental well-being. Adopting a new health regimen or diet can be beneficial.
- **August**: Creativity continues to be a theme. Pursue creative projects and hobbies that bring you joy and fulfillment. Express yourself freely and artistically.
- **September**: Education and learning are highlighted. Enroll in courses or workshops that interest you. It's an excellent time for intellectual expansion.
- **October**: Relationships, both romantic and platonic, are in focus. If single, you might meet someone special. For those in relationships, this is a time to nurture and grow your connection.
- **November**: Reflect on your personal journey and achievements. As your birthday approaches, review the past year and set goals for the coming one.
- **December**: The year ends with a focus on relaxation and rejuvenation. Enjoy the holiday season, and take time to unwind and reflect on the year's journey.

This forecast for Pisces in 2024 suggests a year filled with opportunities for creative expression, personal growth, and deepening emotional connections. Use these astrological insights to navigate the year, embracing the opportunities for development and self-discovery.

As you read through these forecasts, remember that astrology offers guidance and perspective, not definitive answers. The stars provide a map, but the journey is uniquely yours. Use these insights to enhance your understanding of the energies at play each month, and approach the year with confidence and a sense of adventure.

Focus on love, career, health, and personal well-being

Aries (March 21 - April 19)

- **Love**: Opportunities for new romantic encounters and deepening existing relationships, especially in the spring and summer months.
- **Career**: Potential for significant career advancements, particularly around mid-year. Stay proactive in seeking new opportunities.

- **Health**: Importance of balancing physical activity with relaxation to maintain optimal health. Mindfulness practices can be beneficial in managing stress.
- **Well-being**: Self-reflection and personal growth are highlighted throughout the year. Engaging in hobbies and interests that bring joy is crucial.

Taurus (April 20 - May 20)

- **Love**: The year brings a focus on harmonious and stable relationships. The latter half of the year may bring more profound connections.
- **Career**: Opportunities for financial growth and career development, especially in creative fields. Networking is key.
- **Health**: Emphasize a balanced diet and regular exercise. The fall months are ideal for starting new health routines.
- **Well-being**: Mental health should be a priority. Practices like meditation and yoga can provide emotional balance and peace.

Gemini (May 21 - June 20)

- **Love**: A year of dynamic social interactions that could lead to romantic possibilities. Communication in relationships is crucial.
- **Career**: Creative projects and collaborative efforts are favored. Mid-year might bring unexpected career opportunities.

- **Health**: Focus on mental health and maintaining an active social life for overall well-being.
- **Well-being**: Travel and learning new skills can provide a sense of fulfillment and happiness.

Cancer (June 21 - July 22)

- **Love**: Emotional depth in relationships is a theme. The end of the year may bring special moments in personal relationships.
- **Career**: Potential for career growth through nurturing professional relationships. A balanced approach to work and life is essential.
- **Health**: Prioritize self-care and mental health, especially during stressful periods.
- **Well-being**: Home and family life provide comfort and grounding. Engaging in home-based activities can enhance overall happiness.

Leo (July 23 - August 22)

- **Love**: A vibrant social life leads to exciting romantic prospects. Existing relationships may undergo positive transformations.
- **Career**: Leadership roles and creative projects are highlighted. The latter part of the year might offer advancement opportunities.
- **Health**: Regular physical activity is vital to maintain energy levels. Outdoor activities can be particularly beneficial.

- **Well-being**: Expressing creativity and engaging in leisure activities boost happiness and personal satisfaction.

Virgo (August 23 - September 22)

- **Love**: Relationships require open communication and understanding. The spring months are favorable for romance.
- **Career**: A focus on detail and organization leads to professional success. Financial planning is crucial throughout the year.
- **Health**: Stress management and preventive health measures are important.
- **Well-being**: Intellectual pursuits and hobbies that require focus can provide a sense of achievement and mental stimulation.

Libra (September 23 - October 22)

- **Love**: A year for building and strengthening relationships. Late summer and early autumn are particularly favorable for romance.
- **Career**: Collaborative projects and partnerships are successful. Balancing professional and personal life is a key theme.
- **Health**: Emphasis on maintaining a balanced lifestyle and mental well-being.

- **Well-being**: Social activities and cultural events enhance happiness and provide a sense of belonging.

Scorpio (October 23 - November 21)

- **Love**: Deep emotional connections are possible. Late 2024 is significant for romantic developments.
- **Career**: Opportunities for transformation and growth in your career, especially through embracing change.
- **Health**: Intense periods of work require attention to physical health and relaxation.
- **Well-being**: Private time and introspection are vital for personal growth and understanding.

Sagittarius (November 22 - December 21)

- **Love**: Adventure and travel may lead to romantic opportunities. The year is favorable for exploring new relationships or rekindling existing ones.
- **Career**: Opportunities for growth through learning and expansion of skill sets. Late year might bring important career decisions.
- **Health**: Outdoor activities and adventure sports can be beneficial.
- **Well-being**: Exploring new cultures and philosophies contributes to a sense of happiness and fulfillment.

Capricorn (December 22 - January 19)

- **Love**: Stability and commitment in relationships are themes. The year's end could bring significant developments in personal relationships.
- **Career**: Hard work pays off with potential promotions or recognition. Consistency and dedication are key.
- **Health**: Manage stress through mindfulness and time management. Regular exercise is also important.
- **Well-being**: Setting aside time for relaxation and hobbies is essential for a balanced life.

Aquarius (January 20 - February 18)

- **Love**: Open communication and honesty in relationships are important. Mid-year could bring new romantic interests.
- **Career**: Innovative ideas and unique approaches lead to professional success. Collaboration with like-minded individuals is beneficial.
- **Health**: Mental health and social interactions are important for overall well-being.
- **Well-being**: Engaging in community and humanitarian activities provides a sense of purpose and satisfaction.

Pisces (February 19 - March 20)

- **Love**: The year is favorable for deep, soulful connections in relationships. Emotional understanding and empathy are key.

- **Career**: Creative talents can lead to professional opportunities. Mid-2024 is significant for career decisions.
- **Health**: Balance emotional health with physical wellness. Activities like swimming or dance can be especially enjoyable.
- **Well-being**: Artistic expression and spiritual practices enhance personal growth and happiness.

These forecasts provide a general guide for each zodiac sign in 2024, focusing on love, career, health, and well-being. As with any astrological prediction, they are subject to individual interpretation and external factors.

Custom advice for facing challenges and seizing opportunities

Aries (March 21 - April 19)

- **Challenges**: Navigating professional competition; managing impulsiveness.
- **Opportunities**: Leadership roles; initiating new projects.
- **Advice**: Embrace your natural leadership qualities but practice patience and strategic planning.

Taurus (April 20 - May 20)

- **Challenges**: Adapting to change; financial management.
- **Opportunities**: Enhancing personal relationships; career growth in creative fields.
- **Advice**: Stay open to new ideas and be flexible in your approach to both personal and professional life.

Gemini (May 21 - June 20)

- **Challenges**: Maintaining focus; decision-making in relationships.
- **Opportunities**: Networking; creative collaborations.
- **Advice**: Utilize your excellent communication skills to build strong connections and clarify your goals.

Cancer (June 21 - July 22)

- **Challenges**: Balancing work and home life; overcoming emotional insecurities.
- **Opportunities**: Strengthening family bonds; career advancements.
- **Advice**: Prioritize self-care and don't be afraid to express your needs both at home and work.

Leo (July 23 - August 22)

- **Challenges**: Dealing with ego clashes; work-life balance.
- **Opportunities**: Romantic relationships; creative projects.

- **Advice**: Recognize the value of collaboration and the importance of nurturing personal relationships alongside professional ones.

Virgo (August 23 - September 22)

- **Challenges**: Perfectionism; stress management.
- **Opportunities**: Skill development; efficient work methodologies.
- **Advice**: Adopt a more flexible approach and focus on practical solutions without getting lost in details.

Libra (September 23 - October 22)

- **Challenges**: Decision-making; maintaining harmony in relationships.
- **Opportunities**: Building new partnerships; artistic pursuits.
- **Advice**: Trust your instincts when making decisions and seek balance between pleasing others and asserting your needs.

Scorpio (October 23 - November 21)

- **Challenges**: Intense emotions; power struggles in relationships.
- **Opportunities**: Deep emotional connections; transformative personal growth.

- **Advice**: Practice openness and vulnerability in relationships and use your intuition to navigate complex situations.

Sagittarius (November 22 - December 21)

- **Challenges**: Restlessness; overcommitment.
- **Opportunities**: Travel; educational pursuits.
- **Advice**: Focus on setting realistic goals and channel your energy into meaningful adventures and learning.

Capricorn (December 22 - January 19)

- **Challenges**: Workaholism; resistance to change.
- **Opportunities**: Career achievements; financial stability.
- **Advice**: Embrace flexibility and innovation in your career and remember the value of work-life balance.

Aquarius (January 20 - February 18)

- **Challenges**: Feeling misunderstood; maintaining individuality in relationships.
- **Opportunities**: Community involvement; innovative projects.
- **Advice**: Communicate your unique ideas effectively and seek collaborations that align with your values.

Pisces (February 19 - March 20)

- **Challenges**: Emotional sensitivity; setting boundaries.
- **Opportunities**: Artistic expression; spiritual growth.

- **Advice**: Engage in creative activities as an outlet for your emotions and seek connections that are spiritually fulfilling.

These forecasts offer tailored advice for each zodiac sign, helping to navigate the specific challenges and make the most of the opportunities that 2024 brings. Remember, these insights are meant to guide and empower you to make choices that align with your personal journey and growth.

Chapter 3: Love and Relationships

Analyzing Sign Compatibilities for 2024

In 2024, the cosmic dance of the planets brings a unique set of influences to the realm of love and relationships. Understanding the compatibilities between zodiac signs can guide individuals towards more harmonious and fulfilling interactions. This chapter delves into the nuances of these astrological connections, offering insights into the dynamics of various pairings.

Aries and Libra

- **Dynamics**: Aries' boldness harmoniously balances with Libra's quest for harmony. This year emphasizes a blend of passion and diplomacy in their interactions.
- **Challenge**: Aries may find Libra's indecisiveness frustrating, while Libra might feel overwhelmed by Aries' intensity.
- **Strength**: Mutual respect and admiration, with Aries appreciating Libra's fairness and Libra admiring Aries' courage.

Taurus and Scorpio

- **Dynamics**: Their opposite natures create a magnetic attraction. Taurus' stability complements Scorpio's depth in 2024.
- **Challenge**: Taurus' resistance to change may clash with Scorpio's transformative nature.
- **Strength**: A deep, unspoken understanding and a shared value for loyalty and commitment.

Gemini and Sagittarius

- **Dynamics**: Both signs seek intellectual stimulation, making their connection mentally invigorating. 2024 enhances their shared love for adventure and learning.
- **Challenge**: Gemini's fickleness can be at odds with Sagittarius' search for deeper meaning.

- **Strength**: A relationship filled with lively conversations, laughter, and mutual growth.

Cancer and Capricorn

- **Dynamics**: Cancer's emotional depth finds grounding in Capricorn's pragmatism. This year, their bond strengthens as they navigate life's practicalities and emotional landscapes together.
- **Challenge**: Cancer's sensitivity might conflict with Capricorn's stoicism.
- **Strength**: A comforting and supportive partnership, offering a balance of emotional warmth and practical support.

Leo and Aquarius

- **Dynamics**: Leo's flair and Aquarius' uniqueness create a dynamic and unconventional pairing. In 2024, their relationship thrives on mutual respect for each other's individuality.
- **Challenge**: Leo's need for attention may conflict with Aquarius' independent streak.
- **Strength**: A partnership that celebrates creativity, freedom, and respect for personal space.

Virgo and Pisces

- **Dynamics**: Virgo's practicality meshes well with Pisces' dreaminess, creating a balanced and nurturing relationship in 2024.
- **Challenge**: Virgo's criticism can dampen Pisces' spiritual and emotional expressions.
- **Strength**: Complementary strengths, where Virgo offers grounded support, and Pisces brings creativity and empathy.

In 2024, the astrological landscape provides a rich tapestry for exploring love and relationship dynamics. By understanding and embracing the unique qualities of each sign pairing, individuals can foster deeper connections and navigate the waters of romance with greater awareness and empathy.

Nurturing Healthy and Fulfilling Relationships

As the celestial bodies continue their journey through the sky, 2024 brings unique challenges and opportunities in the realm of love and relationships for each zodiac sign. Here is some tailored advice to help nurture healthy and fulfilling relationships throughout the year:

Aries (March 21 - April 19)

- **Advice**: Practice patience and active listening in relationships. Your natural impulsiveness may be tempered by understanding and considering your partner's perspective.

Taurus (April 20 - May 20)

- **Advice**: Embrace flexibility in your relationships. While your desire for stability is strong, be open to new experiences and changes that your partner brings.

Gemini (May 21 - June 20)

- **Advice**: Communication is your strength, but ensure it's a two-way street. Pay attention to your partner's needs and be open in expressing your own.

Cancer (June 21 - July 22)

- **Advice**: Allow vulnerability in your relationships. Sharing your feelings can deepen connections, but also ensure you set healthy boundaries.

Leo (July 23 - August 22)

- **Advice**: Balance your need for attention with your partner's. Show appreciation and make sure your partner feels valued and heard.

Virgo (August 23 - September 22)

- **Advice**: Let go of perfectionism in relationships. Embrace imperfections in both yourself and your partner, and focus on building a supportive and understanding bond.

Libra (September 23 - October 22)

- **Advice**: Seek balance between your needs and those of your partner. Avoid sacrificing your own happiness for the sake of harmony.

Scorpio (October 23 - November 21)

- **Advice**: Trust and openness are key. Work on building trust and don't let jealousy or possessiveness undermine your relationships.

Sagittarius (November 22 - December 21)

- **Advice**: Respect your need for freedom and adventure, but also commit to being present and engaged in your relationships.

Capricorn (December 22 - January 19)

- **Advice**: Make time for your relationships amidst your busy schedule. Show your loved ones that they are a priority through your actions and commitment.

Aquarius (January 20 - February 18)

- **Advice**: While you cherish your independence, remember that sharing and togetherness are also crucial in a relationship. Balance your individuality with your partner's needs.

Pisces (February 19 - March 20)

- **Advice**: Stay grounded and communicate your needs clearly. Your empathy is a gift, but ensure that you don't lose yourself while catering to your partner's needs.

In 2024, every zodiac sign has the opportunity to grow and strengthen their relationships. By understanding and embracing these individualized pieces of advice, you can work towards nurturing healthier, more fulfilling connections with those you love. Remember, relationships are about mutual respect, understanding, and growth, and this year offers the perfect canvas to paint a beautiful love story.

Favorable Periods for New Encounters and Significant Decisions

The cosmic landscape of 2024 presents specific periods that are especially auspicious for forming new romantic encounters or making significant decisions in relationships. Let's explore these favorable periods for each zodiac sign:

Aries (March 21 - April 19)

- **New Encounters**: Mid-March to late April is a vibrant time for Aries to meet someone new, as their charisma and energy are at a peak.
- **Significant Decisions**: Late September to mid-October is ideal for making important relationship decisions, with a focus on commitment and future planning.

Taurus (April 20 - May 20)

- **New Encounters**: Early May brings a heightened sensuality and attractiveness, making it a prime time for Taurus to attract a new partner.
- **Significant Decisions**: Mid-November is a period of stability, where Taurus can make wise decisions about the direction of their relationships.

Gemini (May 21 - June 20)

- **New Encounters**: Late June, when social activities are at a high, offers Gemini the perfect setting to meet someone special.
- **Significant Decisions**: Early August is a time of clarity for Gemini, ideal for making choices about moving forward in a relationship.

Cancer (June 21 - July 22)

- **New Encounters**: Mid-July, Cancer's charm is irresistible, making it a great time to start a new romance.

- **Significant Decisions**: Late October offers a reflective period for Cancer to contemplate the future of their relationships.

Leo (July 23 - August 22)

- **New Encounters**: Early August, when Leo's magnetism is strongest, is perfect for attracting new love interests.
- **Significant Decisions**: In December, Leo can make important relationship decisions with confidence and clarity.

Virgo (August 23 - September 22)

- **New Encounters**: September, particularly around their birthday, is a time of renewal and new beginnings in love for Virgo.
- **Significant Decisions**: Early January 2025 (still relevant for the 2024 astrological cycle) provides a period of practical thinking for Virgo to make key relationship choices.

Libra (September 23 - October 22)

- **New Encounters**: Mid-October, when Libra's allure is at its peak, is a promising time for new romantic interests.
- **Significant Decisions**: Late March 2025 offers a balanced perspective for Libra to make important love-related decisions.

Scorpio (October 23 - November 21)

- **New Encounters**: Early November brings an intense allure to Scorpio, heightening chances for passionate encounters.
- **Significant Decisions**: Mid-February is a time for deep introspection, allowing Scorpio to make insightful decisions about their relationships.

Sagittarius (November 22 - December 21)

- **New Encounters**: Late December, Sagittarius may find themselves embarking on a new romantic journey, as their adventurous spirit attracts potential partners.
- **Significant Decisions**: Early April is a time of optimism and foresight, perfect for Sagittarius to make decisions about their love life.

Capricorn (December 22 - January 19)

- **New Encounters**: January, with the New Year's energy, is a time for Capricorn to meet someone who shares their ambitions and values.
- **Significant Decisions**: Mid-May provides a stable and practical mindset for Capricorn to make lasting relationship choices.

Aquarius (January 20 - February 18)

- **New Encounters**: Late February is a period of openness and social engagement, ideal for Aquarius to form new connections.
- **Significant Decisions**: Late July is a period of self-awareness and insight, helping Aquarius make informed decisions in their relationships.

Pisces (February 19 - March 20)

- **New Encounters**: Early March, Pisces is especially romantic and empathetic, attracting potential partners easily.
- **Significant Decisions**: Mid-September allows Pisces to use their intuition and emotional intelligence to make profound relationship decisions.

The year 2024 is rich with opportunities for all signs to either embark on new romantic journeys or strengthen their existing relationships. Understanding these favorable periods helps in aligning with the cosmic rhythms, potentially leading to more fulfilling love experiences.

Chapter 4: Career and Finance

Forecasts for Career and Financial Advancement

As we navigate through the astrological tides of 2024, the alignment of stars and planets plays a significant role in shaping professional paths and financial landscapes. This chapter offers insights into the potential for career advancement and financial prosperity for each zodiac sign.

Aries (March 21 - April 19)

- **Career**: A year of bold initiatives and leadership. Opportunities to take on new challenges that push you into the limelight.
- **Finance**: Wise investments, especially in personal projects or entrepreneurial ventures, could yield substantial returns.

Taurus (April 20 - May 20)

- **Career**: Steady progress in existing roles. 2024 may not bring drastic changes, but consistent performance leads to recognition and potential promotions.

- **Finance**: Stable financial growth, with an emphasis on saving and building assets. Real estate investments could be favorable.

Gemini (May 21 - June 20)

- **Career**: A year for Geminis to capitalize on their adaptability and communication skills. New partnerships and collaborative projects are likely.
- **Finance**: Diversify your investment portfolio. Unexpected financial gains are possible through networking.

Cancer (June 21 - July 22)

- **Career**: Growth comes from nurturing professional relationships. Opportunities to lead projects that require emotional intelligence and a personal touch.
- **Finance**: Focus on financial security. Long-term investments and savings plans will be beneficial.

Leo (July 23 - August 22)

- **Career**: A chance to shine in your professional life. Creative projects and roles that require leadership will be successful.
- **Finance**: Good year for making investments in the stock market and entertainment industries.

Virgo (August 23 - September 22)

- **Career**: Utilize your analytical skills and attention to detail. Career advancements are likely in fields requiring precision and efficiency.
- **Finance**: A disciplined approach to financial planning pays off. Potential gains from investments in technology and health sectors.

Libra (September 23 - October 22)

- **Career**: Collaborative efforts and partnerships thrive. Diplomacy in the workplace leads to fruitful outcomes.
- **Finance**: Balanced financial planning is key. Look for opportunities in art and design-related fields.

Scorpio (October 23 - November 21)

- **Career**: Intense focus and determination bring success in challenging projects. Potential for a significant career transformation.
- **Finance**: Be cautious with investments. Research thoroughly before committing to financial decisions.

Sagittarius (November 22 - December 21)

- **Career**: A year of exploration and expansion. Opportunities for travel and learning that can enhance your professional life.
- **Finance**: Consider investing in education or travel-related fields. Be mindful of impulsive spending.

Capricorn (December 22 - January 19)

- **Career**: Hard work leads to substantial progress and possible elevation to higher positions. Networking with influential figures is beneficial.
- **Finance**: Strong potential for financial growth. Investments in traditional and stable markets are favored.

Aquarius (January 20 - February 18)

- **Career**: Innovations and unconventional ideas are your keys to success. Look for opportunities in cutting-edge technologies or humanitarian projects.
- **Finance**: Unconventional investments may prove profitable. Stay informed about market trends.

Pisces (February 19 - March 20)

- **Career**: Creative and compassionate roles are favored. Opportunities to work in artistic, healing, or charitable professions.
- **Finance**: Focus on financial planning that aligns with your values. Ethical investments could bring both personal satisfaction and monetary gains.

For each zodiac sign, 2024 presents a unique set of cosmic influences that impact professional endeavors and financial matters. By tuning into these astrological insights, individuals can navigate their career paths and financial decisions with greater awareness and potential for success.

Auspicious Times to Launch Projects or Make Investments

In the ever-shifting cosmic landscape of 2024, certain periods emerge as particularly favorable for initiating new projects or making strategic investments. This chapter highlights these opportune moments for each zodiac sign, aiding in the planning of key career and financial moves.

Aries (March 21 - April 19)

- **Project Launch**: Late March to early April is a power-packed time for Aries to initiate new ventures. Mars brings energy and drive to your endeavors.
- **Investment**: Mid-May offers promising opportunities for investments, especially in sectors that demand innovation and courage.

Taurus (April 20 - May 20)

- **Project Launch**: Early June is ideal for Taurus to start new projects, especially those requiring a steady and methodical approach.
- **Investment**: Late July to early August is an excellent period for making long-term investments, particularly in real estate or traditional markets.

Gemini (May 21 - June 20)

- **Project Launch**: Mid-July presents a window for Gemini to kick off projects that require communication skills and networking.
- **Investment**: Early September is favorable for investments in technology and social media ventures.

Cancer (June 21 - July 22)

- **Project Launch**: Late August is a conducive time for Cancer to begin projects, especially those related to home-based businesses or family ventures.
- **Investment**: Mid-October is optimal for making investments in safe and secure assets.

Leo (July 23 - August 22)

- **Project Launch**: Early September, when your charisma is at its peak, is ideal for Leos to launch creative or entertainment-related projects.
- **Investment**: Late November provides favorable opportunities for investing in the stock market or luxury goods.

Virgo (August 23 - September 22)

- **Project Launch**: Mid-September is a prime time for Virgo to start projects that benefit from your analytical and detail-oriented nature.

- **Investment**: Early December is advantageous for investments in healthcare and service industries.

Libra (September 23 - October 22)

- **Project Launch**: Late October, during Libra season, is perfect for initiating artistic or partnership-based projects.
- **Investment**: Mid-January 2025 presents opportunities for profitable investments, particularly in arts and justice-related fields.

Scorpio (October 23 - November 21)

- **Project Launch**: Early November is a powerful time for Scorpios to begin ventures that require intensity and transformation.
- **Investment**: Late February 2025 is an auspicious period for investments in research and development or mystery-related areas.

Sagittarius (November 22 - December 21)

- **Project Launch**: Mid-December, aligning with your adventurous spirit, is excellent for starting travel or education-related projects.
- **Investment**: Early March 2025 is beneficial for investing in foreign markets or publishing.

Capricorn (December 22 - January 19)

- **Project Launch**: January, with the New Year's energy, is a potent time for Capricorns to start new business ventures or corporate projects.
- **Investment**: Late April is conducive to making investments, especially in traditional industries and government bonds.

Aquarius (January 20 - February 18)

- **Project Launch**: Early February, during Aquarius season, is ideal for innovative projects or technology-related ventures.
- **Investment**: Mid-May is an opportune time for investing in startups or unconventional markets.

Pisces (February 19 - March 20)

- **Project Launch**: Late March, tapping into your creative and empathetic qualities, is perfect for starting artistic or healing projects.
- **Investment**: Early June provides favorable conditions for investments in the arts, spiritual realms, or water-related industries.

For each zodiac sign, 2024 offers specific periods where the stars align favorably for launching new ventures or making wise financial decisions. Timing your actions in sync with these auspicious intervals can enhance the likelihood of success and prosperity in your career and financial endeavors.

Money Management Tips for 2024 Based on Your Zodiac Sign

Navigating the financial waters of 2024 requires a keen understanding of one's astrological influences. Each zodiac sign has unique traits that can be harnessed for effective money management and financial success. This chapter provides tailored tips for each sign to optimize their financial health in the coming year.

Aries (March 21 - April 19)

- **Money Management Tips**: Embrace bold financial moves but avoid impulsiveness. Consider long-term investments and resist the temptation of quick, risky ventures.

Taurus (April 20 - May 20)

- **Money Management Tips**: Your natural inclination towards stability serves you well. Focus on building a solid savings plan and invest in tangible assets like real estate.

Gemini (May 21 - June 20)

- **Money Management Tips**: Diversify your financial portfolio. Your adaptability can lead to success in various investment avenues, but beware of scattering your resources too thinly.

Cancer (June 21 - July 22)

- **Money Management Tips**: Security is key. Invest in safe, long-term options and create a financial safety net. Emotional spending should be monitored closely.

Leo (July 23 - August 22)

- **Money Management Tips**: Balance your generous nature with practical financial planning. Luxurious spending can be tempting, but prioritize investments that bring long-term returns.

Virgo (August 23 - September 22)

- **Money Management Tips**: Utilize your analytical skills for budgeting and financial planning. Detail-oriented approaches to investments can yield fruitful outcomes.

Libra (September 23 - October 22)

- **Money Management Tips**: Avoid indecision in financial matters. Weigh your options carefully but commit to a well-thought-out financial strategy.

Scorpio (October 23 - November 21)

- **Money Management Tips**: Trust your instincts but also do thorough research before making significant financial decisions. Consider investments that offer both growth potential and security.

Sagittarius (November 22 - December 21)

- **Money Management Tips**: Your love for freedom should not translate into reckless financial decisions. Focus on savings plans that allow flexibility but also offer stability.

Capricorn (December 22 - January 19)

- **Money Management Tips**: Your disciplined nature is your biggest asset. Invest in long-term, high-value assets and continually review your financial strategies.

Aquarius (January 20 - February 18)

- **Money Management Tips**: Innovative financial strategies can pay off. Explore unconventional investment opportunities, but ensure they align with your long-term financial goals.

Pisces (February 19 - March 20)

- **Money Management Tips**: Guard against financial idealism. Set practical financial goals and seek professional advice if needed. Consider creative ways to grow your wealth.

For each zodiac sign, 2024 offers unique opportunities and challenges in the realm of finances. By aligning your money management strategies with your astrological strengths and weaknesses, you can navigate the year with greater financial wisdom and potential for prosperity.

Chapter 5: Health and Wellness

Lifestyle and Wellness Tips for 2024 Tailored to Each Zodiac Sign

The year 2024 brings unique health and wellness challenges and opportunities for each zodiac sign. Understanding and aligning with these astrological influences can greatly enhance your overall well-being. This chapter provides specific lifestyle and wellness tips tailored to the needs and tendencies of each sign.

Aries (March 21 - April 19)

- **Lifestyle Tips**: Incorporate high-energy activities like sports or martial arts to channel your natural dynamism.

- **Wellness Tips**: Practice stress-relief techniques such as meditation or yoga to balance your fiery nature.

Taurus (April 20 - May 20)

- **Lifestyle Tips**: Engage in outdoor activities that connect you with nature, like hiking or gardening.
- **Wellness Tips**: Prioritize a balanced diet and regular massage therapy to maintain physical and mental harmony.

Gemini (May 21 - June 20)

- **Lifestyle Tips**: Include social activities in your fitness routine, like group sports or dance classes, to keep engaged.
- **Wellness Tips**: Mental stimulation is crucial; try brain games or puzzles, and ensure ample time for restful sleep.

Cancer (June 21 - July 22)

- **Lifestyle Tips**: Water-based activities such as swimming can be soothing and beneficial for your well-being.
- **Wellness Tips**: Emotional health is key; consider regular journaling or therapy sessions to process feelings.

Leo (July 23 - August 22)

- **Lifestyle Tips**: Regular exercise, particularly cardio workouts, will help maintain your vitality.

- **Wellness Tips**: Adopt a skincare routine that reflects your love for self-care and indulgence.

Virgo (August 23 - September 22)

- **Lifestyle Tips**: Activities that require precision, like yoga or Pilates, suit your detail-oriented nature.
- **Wellness Tips**: Maintain a diet rich in organic foods and consider routine health check-ups.

Libra (September 23 - October 22)

- **Lifestyle Tips**: Engage in aesthetically pleasing fitness activities like dance or ballet to align with your love for beauty.
- **Wellness Tips**: Practice mindfulness and meditation to maintain inner balance and harmony.

Scorpio (October 23 - November 21)

- **Lifestyle Tips**: Intense workouts like HIIT or boxing align well with your passionate nature.
- **Wellness Tips**: Detoxification practices, either dietary or through activities like saunas, can be beneficial.

Sagittarius (November 22 - December 21)

- **Lifestyle Tips**: Adventure sports or outdoor activities align with your explorative spirit.
- **Wellness Tips**: Prioritize flexibility in your diet and exercise routine to suit your need for variety.

Capricorn (December 22 - January 19)

- **Lifestyle Tips**: Structured exercise regimes and disciplined fitness goals are ideal for your ambitious nature.
- **Wellness Tips**: Ensure sufficient relaxation and leisure time to balance your hardworking tendencies.

Aquarius (January 20 - February 18)

- **Lifestyle Tips**: Engage in futuristic fitness trends or technology-based health monitoring.
- **Wellness Tips**: Community-driven wellness activities or group meditation can be fulfilling.

Pisces (February 19 - March 20)

- **Lifestyle Tips**: Gentle, flowing exercises like tai chi or swimming resonate with your fluid nature.
- **Wellness Tips**: Regular creative outlets such as art or music therapy are essential for emotional well-being.

Each sign's path to health and wellness in 2024 is unique, reflecting their individual traits and preferences. By embracing these tailored tips, you can enhance your physical, mental, and emotional health, leading to a more balanced and fulfilling year.

Critical Periods for Health and Prevention Strategies in 2024

Astrology not only guides us in making life decisions but can also be instrumental in predicting and preparing for critical health periods. The year 2024 presents various astrological phases where certain zodiac signs might experience health vulnerabilities. This chapter outlines these critical periods and offers preventive strategies for each sign to maintain optimal health.

Aries (March 21 - April 19)

- **Critical Periods**: Late April and early September.
- **Prevention**: Focus on injury prevention during physical activities. Incorporate relaxation techniques to manage stress and avoid burnout.

Taurus (April 20 - May 20)

- **Critical Periods**: Mid-May and late October.
- **Prevention**: Pay attention to your diet and digestive health. Regular exercise, particularly outdoor activities, will help in maintaining overall well-being.

Gemini (May 21 - June 20)

- **Critical Periods**: Early June and mid-November.

- **Prevention**: Prioritize mental health. Engage in activities that help reduce anxiety, and ensure adequate sleep to support cognitive health.

Cancer (June 21 - July 22)

- **Critical Periods**: Late July and early December.
- **Prevention**: Emotional health is crucial. Practice mindfulness and stress management techniques. Stay connected with loved ones for emotional support.

Leo (July 23 - August 22)

- **Critical Periods**: Mid-August and late December.
- **Prevention**: Monitor heart health and manage stress effectively. Regular cardio exercises and a balanced diet are key to maintaining vitality.

Virgo (August 23 - September 22)

- **Critical Periods**: Early September and mid-January 2025.
- **Prevention**: Gut health is vital. Incorporate a diet rich in fiber and probiotics. Regular medical check-ups are advisable.

Libra (September 23 - October 22)

- **Critical Periods**: Late October and early February 2025.

- **Prevention**: Balance is essential. Avoid overexertion and practice relaxation techniques. Pay attention to kidney and adrenal health.

Scorpio (October 23 - November 21)

- **Critical Periods**: Mid-November and late February 2025.
- **Prevention**: Stay hydrated and maintain a healthy reproductive system. Regular detoxification and practicing safe sex are recommended.

Sagittarius (November 22 - December 21)

- **Critical Periods**: Early December and mid-March 2025.
- **Prevention**: Focus on liver health and maintaining a healthy weight. Moderation in diet and alcohol consumption is crucial.

Capricorn (December 22 - January 19)

- **Critical Periods**: Mid-January and late March 2025.
- **Prevention**: Bone and joint health should be a priority. Calcium-rich diets and regular strength training can be beneficial.

Aquarius (January 20 - February 18)

- **Critical Periods**: Early February and mid-April 2025.

- **Prevention**: Circulatory health is key. Aerobic exercises and avoiding prolonged sitting can help maintain cardiovascular health.

Pisces (February 19 - March 20)

- **Critical Periods**: Late March and early May 2025.
- **Prevention**: Foot care is important. Comfortable footwear and regular foot massages can prevent issues. Also, focus on immune system health.

By being aware of these critical periods and adopting preventive health strategies, each zodiac sign can navigate 2024 with greater confidence in maintaining their health and wellness. Proactive measures and a mindful approach to lifestyle choices will be instrumental in ensuring a healthy year ahead.

The Importance of Mental and Physical Balance in 2024

As we step into 2024, the cosmic energies emphasize the vital importance of maintaining a balance between mental and physical health. This chapter delves into the need for harmonizing the mind and body for each zodiac sign, offering insights and guidance on how to achieve this equilibrium.

Aries (March 21 - April 19)

- **Balance Focus**: Counteract your natural tendency towards physical exertion with mindfulness practices. Meditation and deep-breathing exercises can provide the mental calm needed to balance your energetic disposition.

Taurus (April 20 - May 20)

- **Balance Focus**: Your love for comfort and sensory experiences can be balanced with activities that stimulate the mind. Engage in intellectual pursuits or creative hobbies to complement your physical indulgences.

Gemini (May 21 - June 20)

- **Balance Focus**: As a sign that thrives on mental stimulation, ensure you're also attending to your physical health. Regular exercise, especially outdoor activities, can help ground your mental energy.

Cancer (June 21 - July 22)

- **Balance Focus**: Emotional well-being is crucial for you. Balance this with a consistent physical routine, such as yoga or swimming, which can also help soothe emotional turbulence.

Leo (July 23 - August 22)

- **Balance Focus**: While you naturally focus on physical appearance and vitality, don't neglect your inner world. Practices like journaling or therapy can help you process emotions and achieve mental clarity.

Virgo (August 23 - September 22)

- **Balance Focus**: Your analytical mind benefits from relaxing physical activities. Consider gentle forms of exercise like walking or Tai Chi to create a harmonious mind-body connection.

Libra (September 23 - October 22)

- **Balance Focus**: Achieve balance by combining aesthetic activities with mental challenges. Engage in arts that require both physical involvement and intellectual engagement, like dance or sculpture.

Scorpio (October 23 - November 21)

- **Balance Focus**: Intense emotions are part of your nature. Channel this intensity into physical outlets like martial arts or intense workouts, which can also provide emotional release.

Sagittarius (November 22 - December 21)

- **Balance Focus**: Your adventurous spirit craves physical activity. Balance this with practices that promote mental expansion, like meditation or philosophical studies.

Capricorn (December 22 - January 19)

- **Balance Focus**: Your focus on achievement and discipline in the physical realm should be counterbalanced with leisure activities that relax the mind, like reading or enjoying nature.

Aquarius (January 20 - February 18)

- **Balance Focus**: With a tendency towards intellectual pursuits, it's important to engage in regular physical exercise. Group sports or community-based fitness activities can be particularly beneficial.

Pisces (February 19 - March 20)

- **Balance Focus**: You have a natural inclination towards emotional and spiritual health. Complement this with a physical routine that grounds you, such as hiking or cycling.

For each zodiac sign, 2024 is a year to focus on creating and maintaining a balance between mental acuity and physical health. By acknowledging and addressing the unique needs of both the mind and the body, one can achieve a state of holistic well-being, essential for navigating the challenges and opportunities that the year may bring.

Chapter 6: Personal Transformation and Spiritual Growth

Overcoming Personal Obstacles and Embracing Inner Growth

The year 2024 offers each zodiac sign unique opportunities for personal transformation and spiritual growth. This chapter provides guidance on how to overcome personal obstacles and foster inner growth, tailored to the astrological nuances of each sign.

Aries (March 21 - April 19)

- **Transformation Guidance**: Harness your natural leadership qualities for personal development. Overcome impulsiveness by cultivating patience and empathy.
- **Spiritual Growth**: Engage in activities that challenge your physical and mental boundaries, fostering resilience and self-awareness.

Taurus (April 20 - May 20)

- **Transformation Guidance**: Embrace change and let go of rigid views to allow personal growth. Practice flexibility in both thought and action.

- **Spiritual Growth**: Explore nature-based spiritual practices that connect you with the earth and your own inner stability.

Gemini (May 21 - June 20)

- **Transformation Guidance**: Develop focus and depth in your pursuits. Overcoming scattered energies will lead to significant personal achievements.
- **Spiritual Growth**: Engage in mindful communication and active listening as a path to deeper understanding and connection.

Cancer (June 21 - July 22)

- **Transformation Guidance**: Cultivate emotional resilience. Learning to navigate your emotional landscape skillfully can be transformative.
- **Spiritual Growth**: Practice self-care rituals and explore emotional healing techniques to enhance your intuitive abilities.

Leo (July 23 - August 22)

- **Transformation Guidance**: Balance your need for external validation with self-reflection. Embrace humility and practice self-compassion.
- **Spiritual Growth**: Creative expression can be a powerful tool for spiritual and personal discovery.

Virgo (August 23 - September 22)

- **Transformation Guidance**: Overcome perfectionism by embracing imperfection as part of the human experience. Learn to value progress over perfection.
- **Spiritual Growth**: Incorporate practices like meditation or yoga to connect with a sense of inner peace and acceptance.

Libra (September 23 - October 22)

- **Transformation Guidance**: Develop decisiveness and confidence in your choices. Trusting your intuition can lead to profound personal growth.
- **Spiritual Growth**: Explore artistic or creative outlets as a means of understanding and expressing your inner world.

Scorpio (October 23 - November 21)

- **Transformation Guidance**: Learn to let go of control and embrace vulnerability. This openness can lead to deep transformation and healing.
- **Spiritual Growth**: Delve into practices that explore the depths of the psyche, such as deep meditation or transformative therapy.

Sagittarius (November 22 - December 21)

- **Transformation Guidance**: Cultivate patience and attention to detail. Broadening your focus beyond the immediate horizon can bring new insights.
- **Spiritual Growth**: Travel, either physically or through the mind, can be a path to spiritual enlightenment and self-discovery.

Capricorn (December 22 - January 19)

- **Transformation Guidance**: Balance your ambition with a healthy regard for personal well-being. Embracing rest and leisure can be transformative.
- **Spiritual Growth**: Engage in practices that challenge your materialistic views, like volunteer work or mindfulness.

Aquarius (January 20 - February 18)

- **Transformation Guidance**: Cultivate deeper emotional connections. Overcoming detachment can lead to richer personal interactions.
- **Spiritual Growth**: Group spiritual practices or community service can align with your humanitarian nature and promote growth.

Pisces (February 19 - March 20)

- **Transformation Guidance**: Strengthen boundaries to protect your emotional well-being. Finding a balance between empathy and self-preservation is key.
- **Spiritual Growth**: Engage in artistic or musical pursuits to explore and express your spiritual nature.

For each sign, 2024 is a year to embrace change and growth, both personally and spiritually. By recognizing and working with your unique astrological traits, you can overcome obstacles and embark on a journey of self-discovery and transformation.

Significant Astrological Moments for Personal Transformation

In 2024, the astrological landscape is punctuated with significant moments that offer profound opportunities for personal transformation and spiritual growth. This chapter explores these pivotal astrological events and how each zodiac sign can harness them for deep personal change and enlightenment.

Aries (March 21 - April 19)

- **Astrological Moment**: Mars entering Aries (Mid-May).
- **Transformation Opportunity**: A powerful period for self-assertion and taking bold steps towards personal

goals. Embrace courage and initiate meaningful life changes.

Taurus (April 20 - May 20)

- **Astrological Moment**: Solar Eclipse in Taurus (Late April).
- **Transformation Opportunity**: A time of significant personal revelations and new beginnings. Reflect on your values and consider paths that align more closely with them.

Gemini (May 21 - June 20)

- **Astrological Moment**: Mercury Retrograde in Gemini (June).
- **Transformation Opportunity**: A period for introspection and re-evaluating life choices. Great for refining plans and clarifying personal communication.

Cancer (June 21 - July 22)

- **Astrological Moment**: Venus transiting Cancer (Early August).
- **Transformation Opportunity**: Emphasis on emotional healing and nurturing relationships. A prime time to address and release past emotional wounds.

Leo (July 23 - August 22)

- **Astrological Moment**: Sun conjunct Leo (Late July).

- **Transformation Opportunity**: A surge of energy and confidence. Focus on self-expression and creative pursuits that reflect your true self.

Virgo (August 23 - September 22)

- **Astrological Moment**: New Moon in Virgo (September).
- **Transformation Opportunity**: Ideal for setting new health and wellness goals. Focus on self-improvement and practical steps towards personal growth.

Libra (September 23 - October 22)

- **Astrological Moment**: Jupiter in Libra (Starting October).
- **Transformation Opportunity**: Expansion in personal relationships and social connections. Embrace harmony and seek growth in partnerships.

Scorpio (October 23 - November 21)

- **Astrological Moment**: Solar Eclipse in Scorpio (Late October).
- **Transformation Opportunity**: Intense emotional insights and transformative experiences. Time to embrace change and personal metamorphosis.

Sagittarius (November 22 - December 21)

- **Astrological Moment**: Jupiter in Sagittarius (Mid-December).
- **Transformation Opportunity**: Exploration of personal beliefs and philosophies. A period of learning, travel, and expanding your worldview.

Capricorn (December 22 - January 19)

- **Astrological Moment**: Pluto returning to Capricorn (Late January).
- **Transformation Opportunity**: Deep introspection and transformation in career and public life. Embrace empowerment and redefine your goals.

Aquarius (January 20 - February 18)

- **Astrological Moment**: Saturn entering Aquarius (March).
- **Transformation Opportunity**: Focus on personal responsibility and structuring life. Great time for implementing long-term changes for future stability.

Pisces (February 19 - March 20)

- **Astrological Moment**: Neptune in Pisces (Throughout 2024).
- **Transformation Opportunity**: Heightened intuition and spiritual connection. Embrace creativity and explore your spiritual and artistic sides.

For each zodiac sign, 2024 is a canvas for significant personal and spiritual transformation. These astrological moments offer gateways to profound self-discovery and growth. Embracing these periods with awareness and intention can lead to lasting and meaningful change.

Recommended Meditations and Spiritual Practices for 2024

The journey of personal transformation and spiritual growth is deeply personal and unique to each individual. In 2024, aligning with specific meditations and spiritual practices can help each zodiac sign further their path of self-discovery and inner peace. This chapter provides tailored recommendations for meditative and spiritual exercises suited to the astrological characteristics of each sign.

Aries (March 21 - April 19)

- **Recommended Meditation**: Active or Movement Meditation. Engaging in dynamic meditation practices helps to harness Aries' natural energy.
- **Spiritual Practice**: Martial arts or sports that require focus and discipline, enhancing self-awareness and control.

Taurus (April 20 - May 20)

- **Recommended Meditation**: Nature Meditation. Spending time in natural settings, practicing mindfulness, can ground Taurus and connect them to the earth.
- **Spiritual Practice**: Gardening or forest bathing, allowing for a deeper sense of peace and grounding.

Gemini (May 21 - June 20)

- **Recommended Meditation**: Guided Visualization. This form of meditation can help Gemini focus their mind and explore new ideas.
- **Spiritual Practice**: Journaling or creative writing as a form of self-expression and exploration.

Cancer (June 21 - July 22)

- **Recommended Meditation**: Moon Meditation. Reflecting on the moon's phases can help Cancer connect with their intuition and emotions.
- **Spiritual Practice**: Water rituals, such as baths or swimming, to soothe and cleanse emotional energies.

Leo (July 23 - August 22)

- **Recommended Meditation**: Heart-Centered Meditation. Focusing on the heart space can cultivate love, compassion, and understanding in Leo.
- **Spiritual Practice**: Creative arts like painting or theater as a form of self-expression and connection to the heart.

Virgo (August 23 - September 22)

- **Recommended Meditation**: Mindfulness Meditation. This practice helps Virgo to stay present and mitigate worries about imperfection.
- **Spiritual Practice**: Service to others, such as volunteering, aligns with Virgo's innate desire to help and heal.

Libra (September 23 - October 22)

- **Recommended Meditation**: Balance Meditation. Practices that focus on harmony and equilibrium can benefit Libra's quest for balance.
- **Spiritual Practice**: Partner yoga or dance, emphasizing harmony with others and the environment.

Scorpio (October 23 - November 21)

- **Recommended Meditation**: Deep Transcendental Meditation. This allows Scorpio to explore deeper layers of the psyche and emotional world.
- **Spiritual Practice**: Investigating the mystical and occult for deeper understanding of the unseen forces.

Sagittarius (November 22 - December 21)

- **Recommended Meditation**: Adventure Visualization. Imagining journeys and adventures can satisfy Sagittarius' need for exploration.

- **Spiritual Practice**: Exploring different philosophies and cultures to expand their understanding of the world.

Capricorn (December 22 - January 19)

- **Recommended Meditation**: Mountain Meditation. Visualizing a mountain can instill a sense of stability and perseverance in Capricorn.
- **Spiritual Practice**: Structured spiritual practices like disciplined yoga or meditation routines, reflecting their organized nature.

Aquarius (January 20 - February 18)

- **Recommended Meditation**: Group Meditation. Participating in group meditative practices aligns with Aquarius' communal nature.
- **Spiritual Practice**: Engaging in community service or humanitarian efforts, fostering a sense of unity and contribution.

Pisces (February 19 - March 20)

- **Recommended Meditation**: Creative Visualization. Imagining creative scenarios can help Pisces connect with their artistic and empathetic side.
- **Spiritual Practice**: Art or music therapy, exploring spirituality through creative expression.

For each zodiac sign, adopting these recommended meditations and spiritual practices in 2024 can offer profound avenues for personal growth and spiritual exploration. Embracing these practices can lead to greater self-awareness, inner peace, and a deeper connection with the universe.

Chapter 7: Retrograde Planets and Their Impact on 2024

Explanation of Retrograde Periods of Planets

In astrology, the retrograde motion of planets is a significant event, symbolizing a time of reflection, reassessment, and internal growth. This chapter delves into the retrograde periods of key planets in 2024 and their potential impact on each zodiac sign.

Mercury Retrograde

- **Dates & Impact**: Occurs several times a year, known for causing communication and travel mishaps.
- **Aries**: Time to rethink communication strategies and revisit old ideas.
- **Taurus**: Reflect on financial decisions and reconnect with personal values.
- **Gemini & Virgo**: (Ruled by Mercury) Heightened impact, urging careful communication and reevaluation of plans.

Venus Retrograde

- **Dates & Impact**: A rarer event, focusing on love, beauty, and financial matters.
- **Libra & Taurus**: (Ruled by Venus) Deep introspection about relationships and personal desires.
- **Scorpio**: Reassessing relationship dynamics and emotional investments.

Mars Retrograde

- **Dates & Impact**: Influences energy levels, aggression, and ambition.
- **Aries & Scorpio**: (Ruled by Mars) A period to reconsider actions and desires. Avoid impulsive decisions.
- **Capricorn**: Reflect on career goals and strategies for achievement.

Jupiter Retrograde

- **Dates & Impact**: A time to reassess growth and expansion plans.
- **Sagittarius & Pisces**: (Ruled by Jupiter) Reevaluate beliefs and educational pursuits.
- **Leo**: Consider the balance between personal growth and external success.

Saturn Retrograde

- **Dates & Impact**: Focuses on discipline, responsibility, and structure.
- **Capricorn & Aquarius**: (Ruled by Saturn) Reconsider career paths and long-term goals.
- **Libra**: Reflect on relationships and the structures that support them.

Uranus Retrograde

- **Dates & Impact**: Encourages unconventional thinking and sudden changes.
- **Aquarius**: (Ruled by Uranus) Embrace innovative ideas but prepare for unpredictability.
- **Taurus**: Consider how flexibility can lead to personal growth.

Neptune Retrograde

- **Dates & Impact**: Focuses on dreams, illusions, and spiritual insights.
- **Pisces**: (Ruled by Neptune) A time for deep spiritual exploration and uncovering hidden truths.
- **Virgo**: Reflect on practicality versus dreams; find a balance.

Pluto Retrograde

- **Dates & Impact**: Related to transformation, power dynamics, and deep subconscious issues.

- **Scorpio**: (Ruled by Pluto) Intense self-reflection and transformation.
- **Leo**: Reassess personal power and influence in relationships.

During these retrograde periods in 2024, each zodiac sign is encouraged to embrace introspection and mindful consideration in various aspects of life. Understanding these planetary influences can provide valuable insights into personal growth and decision-making processes.

Retrograde Planets and Their Impact on 2024

Advice on Navigating These Periods

Retrograde planets bring a time of introspection, re-evaluation, and internal shifts. This chapter provides advice on how to navigate these potentially challenging periods in 2024, turning them into opportunities for growth and self-improvement.

Mercury Retrograde

- **Advice**: Double-check communications and travel plans. It's a time to review, reflect, and reassess rather than initiate new projects. Embrace patience and use this period to complete unfinished tasks.

Venus Retrograde

- **Advice**: Reflect on your relationships and values. It's an opportune time to reassess what and who you value, and why. Avoid making drastic changes in relationships or financial investments during this period.

Mars Retrograde

- **Advice**: Exercise caution in expressing anger and initiating confrontations. It's a period to reassess your actions and desires. Focus on strategic planning rather than impulsive actions.

Jupiter Retrograde

- **Advice**: Re-evaluate your goals and aspirations. This period can bring a deeper understanding of what truly matters to you. Expand your horizons through learning and reflection, rather than immediate expansion.

Saturn Retrograde

- **Advice**: Focus on your responsibilities and long-term goals. It's a time to solidify plans and structures, ensuring they are sustainable and aligned with your true path.

Uranus Retrograde

- **Advice**: Be open to internal changes and revelations. This period might bring unexpected shifts in perspective.

It's an opportunity to break free from old patterns that no longer serve you.

Neptune Retrograde

- **Advice**: Pay attention to your intuition and dreams. It's a time for spiritual growth and understanding deeper truths. Be wary of illusions and deception, both from others and self-imposed.

Pluto Retrograde

- **Advice**: Embrace transformation and self-discovery. Deep-seated issues may surface, offering opportunities for healing and empowerment. It's a time to let go of old power dynamics and control issues.

Navigating retrograde periods in 2024 requires mindfulness, patience, and a willingness to embrace inner change. By understanding the unique challenges and opportunities these periods bring, you can use them to foster personal growth, self-awareness, and transformation.

Chapter 8: Key Astral Events of 2024

Eclipses, Conjunctions, and Significant Astral Events

The astral landscape of 2024 presents unique opportunities and challenges for each zodiac sign. Here's how key celestial events will impact each sign.

Aries

- **Solar Eclipse Impact**: A powerful catalyst for personal reinvention and taking bold new directions in your career.
- **Jupiter-Saturn Conjunction**: Brings balance to your professional aspirations and personal life, encouraging prudent yet ambitious goal-setting.

Taurus

- **Lunar Eclipse Impact**: Illuminates financial and emotional stability, pushing you to let go of old security patterns that no longer serve you.
- **Mars-Venus Conjunction**: Highlights the need for harmony in relationships and may spur a passionate new beginning or creative project.

Gemini

- **Grand Trine Impact**: Brings a period of intellectual growth and social connections, enhancing communication skills and networking.
- **T-Square Impact**: Challenges in balancing career, relationships, and personal goals, urging you to find a sustainable middle ground.

Cancer

- **Solar Eclipse Impact**: A pivotal time for emotional and domestic changes. It's ideal for moving, renovating, or making significant family decisions.
- **Lunar Eclipse Impact**: Brings closure to longstanding personal issues, allowing emotional healing and release.

Leo

- **Jupiter-Saturn Conjunction**: Tests the balance between personal expression and responsibilities, encouraging you to find sustainable ways to shine.
- **Grand Trine Impact**: Offers opportunities for creative and romantic expression, bringing joy and fulfillment.

Virgo

- **Mars-Venus Conjunction**: Catalyzes actions towards health and service-oriented goals, blending practicality with passion.

- **T-Square Impact**: May bring work-life balance into focus, requiring careful management of time and resources.

Libra

- **Solar Eclipse Impact**: A chance to redefine your identity and personal goals, especially in partnerships and legal matters.
- **Lunar Eclipse Impact**: Culmination in relationship dynamics, providing clarity and possibly ending unhealthy patterns.

Scorpio

- **Mars-Venus Conjunction**: Intensifies your emotional and romantic life, prompting deep, transformative relationship experiences.
- **Solar Eclipse Impact**: Signals a time of internal transformation, urging you to explore your subconscious and hidden talents.

Sagittarius

- **Jupiter-Saturn Conjunction**: Brings a focus on expanding your horizons while staying grounded in reality, possibly through travel or education.
- **Grand Trine Impact**: Enhances your natural optimism and adventurous spirit, offering new opportunities for growth.

Capricorn

- **T-Square Impact**: Career and home life may be at odds, demanding strategic planning and compromise to navigate challenges.
- **Lunar Eclipse Impact**: A time for re-evaluating career paths and life direction, bringing insights into long-term ambitions.

Aquarius

- **Solar Eclipse Impact**: Opens new avenues in your intellectual pursuits and communication, ideal for starting new studies or writing projects.
- **Jupiter-Saturn Conjunction**: Encourages balancing innovative ideas with practical implementation, especially in community projects.

Pisces

- **Lunar Eclipse Impact**: Emphasizes spiritual and emotional growth, guiding you to let go of past baggage and embrace healing.
- **Neptune's Influence**: Heightens your intuitive and artistic abilities, encouraging you to explore creative and spiritual depths.

For each sign, these celestial events of 2024 are not just mere occurrences but gateways to deeper understanding and personal growth. Embracing these moments with awareness and adaptability can lead to profound transformations and achievements.

Key Astral Events of 2024 for Zodiac Signs

Tips for Making the Most of These Astral Influences (With Dates)

2024's astral landscape is rich with significant events. Here's how each sign can utilize these dates for personal and spiritual growth:

Aries

- **Solar Eclipse (April 8th)**: Embrace new starts by setting audacious goals. Launch initiatives or reinvent aspects of your life.
- **Mars Conjunction (August 14th)**: Channel your heightened energy into productive pursuits. Avoid impulsiveness, focus on strategy.

Taurus

- **Lunar Eclipse (May 26th)**: Reflect on personal and financial security. Ideal for releasing outdated habits and embracing new financial strategies.
- **Venus Retrograde (July 22nd - September 3rd)**: Reassess relationships and values. Deepen connections with loved ones.

Gemini

- **Mercury Retrograde (February 6th - March 3rd, June 7th - July 1st, October 21st - November 13th):** Slow down and carefully manage communication. Revise and refine ideas.
- **Grand Trine (Date varies):** Utilize this harmonious period for networking and strengthening social ties.

Cancer

- **Solar Eclipse (April 8th):** Focus on home and family. Ideal for significant domestic changes or addressing family issues.
- **Lunar Eclipse (May 26th):** Let go of emotional burdens. Practice self-care and nurturing.

Leo

- **Sun Conjunction (August 11th):** Shine in personal and professional life. Pursue creative activities and express your true self.
- **Jupiter Retrograde (September 4th - December 30th):** Reflect on growth and expansion. Align personal development with long-term goals.

Virgo

- **Mercury Retrograde (Dates as above):** Organize and streamline routines. Good time for health check-ups and wellness revisions.

- **Saturn Retrograde (June 17th - November 4th)**: Strengthen structures and routines to support long-term aspirations.

Libra

- **Venus Retrograde (Dates as above)**: Reflect on inner harmony and relationship balance. Seek inner peace.
- **Jupiter-Saturn Conjunction (Date varies)**: Balance relationships with personal growth. Seek equilibrium between partnership and independence.

Scorpio

- **Mars Retrograde (October 30th - January 12th, 2025)**: Reflect on desires and assertiveness. Avoid hasty decisions in conflicts.
- **Pluto Retrograde (April 27th - October 8th)**: Embrace deep transformation. Explore your psyche for hidden truths and strengths.

Sagittarius

- **Jupiter Retrograde (Dates as above)**: Revisit beliefs and knowledge. Seek wisdom that aligns with your current path.
- **Solar Eclipse (April 8th)**: Embrace new philosophies and learning. Expand your horizons.

Capricorn

- **Saturn Retrograde (Dates as above)**: Assess career and long-term goals. Adjust to align with true objectives.
- **Pluto Retrograde (Dates as above)**: Embrace transformative changes in your professional life. Release outdated ambitions.

Aquarius

- **Uranus Retrograde (August 24th - January 1st, 2025)**: Prepare for unexpected changes. Remain flexible and open-minded.
- **Saturn Conjunction (Date varies)**: Structure innovative ideas into actionable plans. Bring unique visions to life.

Pisces

- **Neptune Retrograde (June 28th - December 3rd)**: Explore your spiritual and creative self. Engage in arts and meditation for self-discovery.
- **Lunar Eclipse (May 26th)**: Release old dreams and illusions. Ground aspirations in reality.

These dates provide a roadmap for each sign to harness celestial influences for growth and transformation in 2024. Embracing these moments with awareness and intention can lead to profound personal and spiritual development.

Chapter 9: Overcoming Misfortune in 2024

Lucky Numbers, Days, and More for Each Zodiac Sign

In 2024, each zodiac sign can harness specific elements like lucky numbers, days, and additional practices to enhance their fortune and overcome potential misfortunes. This chapter provides insights into these aspects for each sign.

Aries (March 21 - April 19)

- **Lucky Number**: 9
- **Lucky Day**: Tuesday
- **Fortune Enhancer**: Engaging in competitive activities. This boosts Aries' natural leadership and vitality.
- **Overcoming Misfortune**: Wear red to harness Mars energy, increasing courage and warding off negativity.

Taurus (April 20 - May 20)

- **Lucky Number**: 6
- **Lucky Day**: Friday
- **Fortune Enhancer**: Investing in fine arts or luxury items. This aligns with Taurus's appreciation for beauty and quality.
- **Overcoming Misfortune**: Carrying a rose quartz can attract love and harmony, balancing Venus's influence.

Gemini (May 21 - June 20)

- **Lucky Number**: 5
- **Lucky Day**: Wednesday
- **Fortune Enhancer**: Socializing and networking. Gemini thrives in communicative settings.
- **Overcoming Misfortune**: Carrying agate stones can help in staying grounded and focused.

Cancer (June 21 - July 22)

- **Lucky Number**: 2
- **Lucky Day**: Monday
- **Fortune Enhancer**: Spending time near water. This soothes Cancer's emotional nature.
- **Overcoming Misfortune**: Keeping a moonstone enhances intuition and brings emotional balance.

Leo (July 23 - August 22)

- **Lucky Number**: 1
- **Lucky Day**: Sunday
- **Fortune Enhancer**: Creative endeavors or public performances. This allows Leo's natural charisma to shine.
- **Overcoming Misfortune**: Gold jewelry or accessories can attract positivity and success.

Virgo (August 23 - September 22)

- **Lucky Number**: 4

- **Lucky Day**: Wednesday
- **Fortune Enhancer**: Engaging in activities that require detail and precision, like puzzles or crafts.
- **Overcoming Misfortune**: Carrying or wearing jade can promote wisdom and tranquility.

Libra (September 23 - October 22)

- **Lucky Number**: 7
- **Lucky Day**: Friday
- **Fortune Enhancer**: Participating in artistic or musical events, which align with Libra's refined tastes.
- **Overcoming Misfortune**: Wearing opal can bring balance and harmony, enhancing Libra's Venusian qualities.

Scorpio (October 23 - November 21)

- **Lucky Number**: 8
- **Lucky Day**: Tuesday
- **Fortune Enhancer**: Delving into mysteries or occult studies. This stimulates Scorpio's investigative nature.
- **Overcoming Misfortune**: Black crystals like obsidian can offer protection and absorb negative energies.

Sagittarius (November 22 - December 21)

- **Lucky Number**: 3
- **Lucky Day**: Thursday

- **Fortune Enhancer**: Traveling or exploring new philosophies. This expands Sagittarius's horizons.
- **Overcoming Misfortune**: Carrying turquoise can attract good fortune and protect during travels.

Capricorn (December 22 - January 19)

- **Lucky Number**: 10
- **Lucky Day**: Saturday
- **Fortune Enhancer**: Setting long-term goals and working diligently towards them. This aligns with Capricorn's ambitious nature.
- **Overcoming Misfortune**: Garnet or dark onyx can offer extra strength and resilience.

Aquarius (January 20 - February 18)

- **Lucky Number**: 11
- **Lucky Day**: Saturday
- **Fortune Enhancer**: Engaging in group activities or humanitarian efforts. This satisfies Aquarius's community-oriented spirit.
- **Overcoming Misfortune**: Amethyst can enhance Aquarius's innovative ideas and protect against unforeseen issues.

Pisces (February 19 - March 20)

- **Lucky Number**: 9
- **Lucky Day**: Thursday

- **Fortune Enhancer**: Artistic pursuits such as painting or music. This nurtures Pisces's creative and empathetic nature.
- **Overcoming Misfortune**: Wearing sea-green stones like aquamarine can bring peace and clarity.

For each zodiac sign, these elements can serve as tools to attract fortune and deflect misfortune in 2024. Embracing these practices along with a positive mindset can open doors to new opportunities and experiences.

Chapter 10: Conclusion

Embracing 2024 with a Proactive Approach

Summary of the Year and Encouragement for a Proactive Approach

As we conclude our journey through the astrological insights for 2024, it's clear that this year is marked by significant celestial events, each bringing its unique opportunities and challenges. From the transformative eclipses to the powerful retrogrades, 2024 is a year of profound personal growth and self-discovery.

Aries to Pisces: A Year of Growth

- **Aries**: A year to take bold steps and embrace leadership.
- **Taurus**: Emphasis on financial wisdom and embracing change.
- **Gemini**: Communication and networking take the forefront.
- **Cancer**: Focus on emotional wellbeing and family matters.
- **Leo**: A time to shine in personal and professional spheres.
- **Virgo**: Health and service are your paths to fulfillment.
- **Libra**: Relationships and balance are your guiding stars.
- **Scorpio**: Deep emotional and spiritual transformation awaits.
- **Sagittarius**: Expand your horizons through learning and travel.
- **Capricorn**: Ambition meets practicality in your journey to success.
- **Aquarius**: Innovative ideas and community involvement are key.
- **Pisces**: Spiritual and creative exploration will guide you.

Embracing a Proactive Approach

- **Seize Opportunities**: Each zodiac sign will encounter unique opportunities. Being proactive in recognizing and embracing these moments is crucial.

- **Learn from Challenges**: The challenges of 2024 are not setbacks but stepping stones to greater understanding and personal development.
- **Stay Adaptable**: Flexibility and adaptability are essential. Stay open to the twists and turns of the astrological influences.
- **Cultivate Positivity**: Maintain a positive mindset. It's the fuel that will keep you moving forward through the year's ups and downs.
- **Connect and Share**: Build and rely on your support networks. Sharing your journey and learning from others is invaluable.

As we embrace 2024, let's do so with a proactive spirit, ready to take on the lessons and gifts it has to offer. With the stars as our guides, we can navigate this year with wisdom, courage, and optimism, making it a memorable chapter in our lives.

Awareness and Personal Growth through Astrology in 2024

As we reflect on the astrological journey of 2024, the overarching theme resonates deeply with the importance of self-awareness and personal growth. Astrology, in its unique and mystical way, offers a mirror to our inner selves, providing insights that go beyond the surface of our daily lives.

The Role of Astrology in Self-Discovery

- Astrology is not just a tool for predicting future events; it's a pathway to understanding our deeper selves, our motivations, and our potential. The alignment of stars and planets can offer profound insights into our character, strengths, weaknesses, and life patterns.
- By observing the movements and positions of celestial bodies, we can gain a better understanding of the energies influencing our lives. This understanding allows us to navigate our journey more consciously and intentionally.

Personal Growth through Astrological Guidance

- The key astral events of 2024 – from eclipses to planetary retrogrades – are not mere occurrences but signposts guiding us towards personal evolution. They prompt us to question, reflect, and grow.
- Each zodiac sign has its unique set of challenges and opportunities as laid out in the cosmos. Embracing these can lead to significant growth and development.

Self-Awareness as a Path to Empowerment

- Astrology encourages a deeper level of self-awareness. Understanding our astrological makeup can empower us to make choices that are in harmony with our true nature.

- This self-awareness helps in recognizing our patterns – both constructive and destructive. It guides us in making informed decisions, improving relationships, and pursuing goals that align with our authentic selves.

A Year of Transformation and Enlightenment

- 2024 is poised to be a transformative year, a time for each of us to embrace the wisdom of the stars. It calls for an inward journey, a quest to understand our deepest desires and fears.
- By engaging with astrology, we embark on a path of enlightenment, learning to harness the energies of the universe in a way that fosters growth, healing, and transformation.

In conclusion, 2024 offers a celestial roadmap to each individual, guiding us towards greater self-awareness and personal growth. By understanding and working with the astrological influences of the year, we can unlock our potential and navigate life with greater wisdom and clarity.

How to Use the Horoscope for Personal Planning in 2024

Understanding Your Horoscope

- **Know Your Sun, Moon, and Rising Signs**: Begin by understanding not just your Sun sign (the zodiac sign you typically identify with based on your birth date) but also your Moon and Rising signs. Each provides a layer of insight into your personality, emotions, and how others perceive you.
- **Read the General Trends**: Start with the broader trends for your Sun sign. This will give you an overall picture of the year's energies and how they might affect you.

Integrating Astrology into Personal Planning

- **Align with Planetary Movements**: Plan your key activities around significant astrological events. For instance, start new projects during a New Moon or plan for reflection during a Mercury Retrograde.
- **Utilize Your Lucky Days and Numbers**: Consider scheduling important meetings or events on your lucky days. Incorporate your lucky numbers in daily life for added positive energy.

Using Monthly and Yearly Predictions

- **Monthly Forecasts**: Use monthly forecasts for short-term planning. They can guide you on when to push forward and when to take a step back.
- **Yearly Outlook**: The yearly overview provides a broader perspective, helping you to set long-term goals aligned with the astrological climate.

Balancing Astrological Guidance with Practicality

- **Combine Astrology with Real-World Planning**: While astrology can provide valuable insights, balance this with practical considerations of your daily life.
- **Stay Flexible and Adaptable**: Astrology offers guidance, but it's crucial to remain adaptable to life's unpredictable nature.

Reflecting and Adapting

- **Regular Reflections**: Regularly reflect on how the astrological influences are playing out in your life. Adjust your plans accordingly.
- **Stay Open to Learning**: Use astrology as a tool for self-discovery and growth. Be open to learning and adapting as you go along.

By using astrology as a guide in 2024, you can make informed decisions and plan your year in a way that aligns with the cosmic energies. This approach can help you harness the positive aspects of the year and navigate any challenges more effectively.

www.ingramcontent.com/pod-product-compliance
Lightning Source LLC
Chambersburg PA
CBHW071003080526
44587CB00015B/2331